Speech Minus Applause

Speech Minus Applause

poems

Jim Peterson

Press 53
Winston-Salem

Press 53, LLC
PO Box 30314
Winston-Salem, NC 27130

First Edition

Copyright © 2019 by Jim Peterson

All rights reserved, including the right of reproduction in whole or in part in any form except in the case of brief quotations embodied in critical articles or reviews. For permission, contact publisher at editor@Press53.com, or at the address above.

Cover Art, "Leg," 26" x 16" oil on linen
© 2018 by Jim Muehlemann
used by permission of the artiest

Cover design by Kevin Morgan Watson and Christopher Forrest

Author Photo by Harriet Peterson

Library of Congress Control Number
2018966770

Printed on acid-free paper
ISBN 978-1-941209-97-4

As always, for Harriet, my Whirlwind.

Also for my beloved sister Gayle,

and for all the ones we have lost.

Acknowledgments

My thanks to the editors of the publications in which these poems first appeared:

Flock: "The Thing I Want to Say," "One Wish," "Learning to Speak"

I-70 Review: "Speech Minus Applause," "In Defense of Permanence"

Original Face (Gunpowder Press 2015): "The Grip"

The Bob and Weave (Red Hen Press 2006): "Mentor"

With gratitude to my poet friend Grant Kittrell, whose close readings of this manuscript and suggestions for revision were most helpful. And with thanks to Press 53 editor Christopher Forrest for the kind of attention to a manuscript that makes a real difference.

In addition, I'd like to thank my long time friend and fellow poet Clint McCown for his help and advice over the years. Finally, I want to thank Kevin Watson for the great work he does for so many writers and their books at Press 53.

Contents

Prologue

    The Thing I Want to Say   xiii

Homage to Elmwood Avenue

1	3
2	4
3	5
4	6
5	7
6	8
7	9
8	10
9	11
10	12

Whirlwinds

The Argument	15
My New Friend	16
Fun	17
Mentor	18
Mud	19
The Future	20
Whirlwind	21
The Still Alive	22
The Niche	23
Wild Man	24
Bullets	26
One Wish	28
Seizure	29
In the Flesh	31
The Grip	37
Learning to Speak	39

The Lairs

Your White Shoes	43
The Garden	45
Dead Ringer	46
Mr. Reflex Man	49
Headless	50

Let it Come	51
Hooks	52
Lines of Sight	54
At Night	56
Speech Minus Applause	57
The Lairs	58
The Final Days	59
In Defense of Permanence	60
Prelude to a Move	61
Karma	64
What You Know	66
The Way It Is	68

Epilogue

Minerals	71
About the Artist	73
About the Author	75

I do not say these things for a dollar,
or to fill up the time while I wait for a boat...

—Walt Whitman, *Song of Myself*, Section 47

Prologue

The thing I want to say

is alive
and has no mouth. Once out
it lies like a disembodied
tongue on a plate, no, like
the light from mansions
licking the lake at midnight.
Still, it rises up
in me again and again
and I speak, hanging
my words like ornaments
on the random limbs of trees.
The breeze moves them
a little, and the light falls
off them like rain. It's raining.
The leaves hiss and sigh.
Two dogs on the corner yawn
as if they've heard it all before.
A cat half in and half out
of the gutter is so still
approaching storms
change course. Is that true?
Let me try this again: there is
something in me that dreams
it knows and wants to speak.
Who am I to say it doesn't. Know,
I mean. Who am I to deny
the veracity of an impulse.
I think I am the dream
and the dreamer, but those
are only thoughts. They hang
like drool from my bottom lip.
Everything I say is only like.
The thing I want to say
turns out to be truly nothing.
If that were only true.

Homage to Elmwood Avenue

Improvisations and Juxtapositions

1

It undulates and curves down toward Black Water Creek
ending in the abandoned grounds of an Oddfellows home
for the old. Feeble and infirm, they once strolled, rolled
in wheelchairs, or shuffled behind walkers along the avenue
from which they could not escape, for the avenue
is as much death as it is life. Dispersed now, relocated
to other humble institutions, or into the homes of their
children, loved and despised, they no longer haunt
the neighborhood. I miss them sometimes, the intensity
of their strangeness brought about by decades of being alive.

*

At three a.m. I confuse my hallway to the bathroom
with a dream about a great bridge across a river.
Its brick arches slowly crumble into the current

that washes over the surface where I walk bare-footed
and cold. Have the pipes burst, do I need to call

a plumber? Holes open up and clusters of trout
tread water as if begging for scraps. The farmer's market
sparkles on the opposite bank. I could buy bread

and roll it into little balls. I could cut my arms
and offer my blood to the starving brood. But I

don't know that they are worth it, the way their gills
pulse like noteless accordions, the way their eyes
call me to the deep plunge of a headlong laugh. Move,

I tell myself, longing to reach the head and take a piss.
Smoke curls up from the market chimneys. I can hear

the voices bartering for fish that lie in their beds
of salt. The torrent grabs my shins, and I cannot take
another step, caught between the bank of my bed

and the urgency to buy. I flush the toilet. The current
reverses, carries me like a twig down the eternal hall.

2

No route is straight in this big town, unless it's the path
to your next-door neighbor's house. Built on the bluffs
and hills rising from the James River, plunging into gorges
and climbing back out again, the town's thoroughfares
circle, sidestep, and otherwise avoid, or at least delay
arrival at any destination. The one mile of a crow's flight
is five for the likes of you or me. This is the pleasure
of the place, the frustration of it, the way it holds us
on the crest or in the nadir of our daily lives. Friends
and enemies alike, even strangers, must climb and plummet.

*

When the yard worker completes his tasks,
his fingers thick and tough as the limbs
of a young maple, the grackles and squirrels
return to choice kernels of corn strewn
on the lawn. They mingle without concern,

each one serving only itself, the other so
naturally alien it is no threat. As a kid I visited
a ranch where cattle roamed thousands
of acres. Spooked by a rattler, my old horse
threw me miles from any season I had known.

The sun bore down heavy on my hatless
crown. An island of rimrock offered shifting
slivers of shade. An eagle circling overhead
watched me crawling with objective eyes.
The sharp warning whistle of a marmot

ricocheted among the oblong stones standing
like the ruins of ancient tombs. I studied
an empty bottle of Orange Crush for three hours.
An old cowboy found me, swung me like another
cold draft up behind his oiled and creaking saddle.

3

Have you noticed that major arteries are fed by tributaries
which in their turn are fed by smaller ones until the process
becomes so minute we can no longer observe it? It continues
beneath the surface of our skin, our thoughts. A sidewalk
connects my front door with Elmwood. If anyone wants
to see me, they must travel this path. When the bell rings,
whether enemy or friend, my dog erupts, plunges through
her own small door to harass through the front yard fence. I cannot
deny her her sense of purpose. Still, people arrive at my door.
I cannot deny them their reasons for being. Or me, my own.

*

I draw my curtains wider to see more of the dusk.
The leaves of trees and shrubs hold still
in the reddish light like rust clinging to the air.
Today, I stay inside. Spring has turned suddenly cold.
Like a photograph of a shore, nothing moves in me.
But something like a dream wants to come in.
And something like a gasp wants to go out.
I wish I had work I wanted to do. I wish I could wear
a hood and hang out with the gang of boys
on the corner smoking each cigarette like a statement,

dreaming each simple knife into a complicated blade.
But the nothing of this day gleams in the vivid absence
of light. I make a mental note to myself: keep
breathing, let the tide come in, let it go out. Turn off
the lamp and learn to listen: the silence is almost complete.
A robin outside my window shakes the cold drizzle
from its wings. I pray for something new to do—
to be. I court the sweet stillness settling in my joints
and bones. I could go to the bank and move my money
around. No. Just sit, let this moment die a natural death.

4

When I swing my door open, through plexiglass I meet them
eye to eye—the black gentleman in a dark suit standing next
to his wife dressed for church, wanting me to read and consider
a pamphlet explaining the terrors of modern life, the necessity
of belief and salvation, the imminence of the second coming.
We know each other and we talk and I accept their pamphlet
but don't invite them in. They want to turn me around,
they want to change my life. They refuse to believe me
when I say I have heard it all before. Not this, they say,
reaching out with more literature. I have heard it all before.

*

If I sit here long enough thinking of nothing,
horizons stack up behind my closed lids
like mountain ranges. Vertical arteries of light
stream in and intersect. If I'm not careful,
I dream of blue planets gathering like stray cats
around an old woman who scatters leftovers
in her back yard, crows lighting on fence posts.
I open my eyes, open my window, let the air
flow through my brain like the wind in the tops
of winter pines. But the blue strangers have
already arrived. They make me feel present
to myself, a pocket within a pocket, a face
within a face, two hands meeting each other
under the table. Neither deep nor shallow,
the grave of the mind is limitless space that
nevertheless flexes like a maze of elbows joining
humeri to the splits of radii and ulnae flowing
into hands joining, never mind the bandages
and the scars and the lies. Dig up the long bone
of the axe and test the heft of it in both hands.

5

When I swing the door open, a neighbor wants to give me
some apples. She has too many for herself. A neighbor
hands me a flier for a neighborhood party. A teenage boy
wants me to hire him to mow my lawn, clean my gutters,
trim my trees. A friend stops by. If the weather is good,
we sit on the porch, or in the yard, otherwise we relax
in the living room over a cup of coffee or a glass of Jack.
We talk of the tributaries of love and loss and grief and work
and injustice and joy and hope and compassion and truth
and religion and politics and hope again and again, and death.

*

When I opened my door and stepped out
a chorus of silences greeted me,
a cardinal stalled on the cherry tree limb,

the surface of puddle water smoothed
by the absence of moving air, the interrupted

angle of the diving hawk, hovering now as if

hung by a wire, the windows across the street
darkened, the swallow in my throat arrested
like a child on the threshold of seeing

the forbidden room. The nape of my neck
sprang hairs to the stillness. I wanted

what was in my throat to get over the hump.

I wanted the day to begin again, the wind
to bend the tops of forgotten trees, the hawk
to pluck a stunned robin from the sky.
My neighbors' curtains parted and a boy's

gaze met mine and held, another missing voice

joining the strange hymn like another feather
scattered in the grass. My thoughts were the only
sound, his eyes the only betrayal of the dream.

6

On the avenue lives a doctor with his long driveway
to a grandiose house back among the trees, a lawyer
of international importance, several college professors,
a social worker, an insurance agent, a local tv news anchor,
a carpenter, a cop, a cook, and even husband and wife
shamans, praying over their mesas, conjuring their allies
from the spirit world who help them get what they want—
the healing of a friend, fame and fortune. Sometimes a poor
man or woman shambles down these sidewalks, engages
the trail into the Black Water Creek woods, and disappears.

*

I am not a good man today. Words
catch in my throat like pieces of food
I swallowed wrong. I'd like to take

a walk, I'd like to whistle back at the birds
but I can't shape the air through my lips
the right way. I feel more like an embryo

than like a man, full-fledged, able to laugh
or weep at the correct occasion. Instead,
I only start to speak, only start to lift

an apple and bring it to my teeth. I loom
over the chairs and tables in my house,
I lurk over the dog's bowl that refills

itself—yet another late-night invention
that opens the groaning gate of obsolescence.
I walk outside where the sun beats down

with another day. The neighborhood desert
stretches for miles of rows of houses.
The tablet I discover in my hand is as blank

as the curtained windows of nearby homes.
My way or the highway, I think, and begin to walk.

7

When I leave the avenue, I often seek out the destroyed
and abandoned. The castle ruins of Wales and England.
The ancient temples, pyramids, and battlements of Peru.
Colonial prisons for the indigenous that move deeper
and deeper underground into smaller and smaller rooms
with little air and no light. The Anasazi city of Chaco Canyon
with its maze of multiple-storied lodges and its hundred
sacred kivas. The Puebloan cliff dwellings and petroglyphs
of Mesa Verde. Returning, I sense the bones and relics of ancient
native ones who lie in layer after layer beneath the avenue.

*

I ducked into the cave,
let my backpack fall

and watched the rain
pour over the mouth,
a shade darkening

the ground, the cliffs.
The new-born wind,

rushing and swirling,
blew like fire through
the canyon. I tried

to ignore the pain
in my knee that spread

like a city into suburban
thigh. Jacket as pillow,
I slept for an hour in the white

noise of the downpour,
carving animals

never seen before
on stone walls, building
fires I would never feel.

8

Some of us on the avenue are old and retired. Some of us
are infants barely able to stand or take a step holding
mother's hand. Some of us in the middle are working hard
to stay alive and keep the family whole. Some are young
men who never left home, selling drugs on the corner now,
riding our scooters and bikes to feel the wind on our lost faces.
Some of us take walks in the afternoon to get our exercise,
to visit neighbors, to see and be seen. Our yards are mostly
manicured, though some are growing wild, like we are, behind
our windows and doors, letting go of what we might have been.

*

Outside my window, tree shadows flickered
over the pickup truck in late afternoon sun.
The wind was having fun up there, throwing
the small stems of its stories, the pink blossoms

of its plots, down on the lawn, down into the empty
bed and onto the shingled roofs. I walked outside
to feel the debris that gives the wind its bite
on my face, to feel the sunlight laying down

its last shadows of the day, turning corners and not
coming back. What did this kind of telling stories
have to do with me hiding inside my scenarios
like the rooms of a private hotel? I walked

into the field and found the skull of a mole, light
as a puff of smoke. In the woods, a deer trail
snaked among the knees of trees, the tall
loblolly trunks dialoguing like the legs

of crickets down in the grass. Was it the yellow
pollen—the true climax of this story—that caught
in my throat? Or was it the way the story included
me, a spiral within a spiral in the underbrush?

9

One of us on the avenue is a corgi. One of us is a standard
poodle, two miniatures. Two of us are bulldogs strolling at our
mistress's side. Five of us are Pekinese on leashes like sled dogs
mushing for our master on the blacktop. Two of us are black labs.
Some of us lunge against the plexiglass door when strangers pass.
Some of us, left alone in our kenneled rooms, bark all day. Some of us
in yards bark at falling leaves, pedestrians, clouds overhead, wind
in the canopies, the inkling of a thought arising in our canine brains.
Some of us are cats, purring on a couch, or feral hiding
in the woods by night, slinking under the bird feeders by day.

*

The weather unfolds way up there, breaks like a slow wave

and then settles onto the continents, around the mountains
and oceans and rivers, and finally, for me anyway,

around my fenceposts, my motorcycle handlebars, penetrating
the screen door. I used to consult my computer to know,
but now I let the weather come to me and speak in its own voice,

the sound of the air in my alleyway if I can be alone enough
there to listen and hear, the pressure of its cords against
my window panes. Like weather, I cloud the spoon with breath
before I consume my cereal, transform the space around me

with my heat and scent. The scratch from my bicycle accident

festers, awaits the bluster of sleeplessness. I am a weather
unto myself—a rain, a wind, a burning sun. I walk down

a nearby street full of houses and their hidden storms,
finally to arrive at an enclave in a neighbor's garden,
a table with the drinks already mixed and poured,

the hot and cold of conversation, the purple flowers
of his crepe myrtles taking care of the light overhead. I drink
a climate change, feel it enter the corridors of my body and mind,
like sap in the green veins of that brown leaf on the ground.

10

All is well on the avenue, except those things that can never
be well. Someone fell down the stairs and broke her leg.
Someone's husband, someone's wife, died of cancer. Both grief
and joy hover in the air. Someone's joke was racist. Someone's
daughter gave birth to a baby girl. A child wept. Someone made
a million dollars and will never be the same. Very few of us
will ever ask, Who am I? Why am I doing what I'm doing?
Am I even the one doing it? Meanwhile, the lawnmower
next door will be at it for an hour. My carpet is full of dog hair.
Faces make faces at me from the wall. I am one of them.

Whirlwinds

The Argument

    for Jerry

He said this wasn't exactly
desert, but it would do.

Hip-high sage made a maze.
He chose and chose
and I followed close behind,
sometimes walking beside him
when space allowed.
He juggled the two sides
of our argument
like the small white knuckle-bones
he always carried
from the game he played as a child.

Nighthawks strummed the air above him.
Thrashers sprang away from his steps
like sparks from a strike of stones.

We got separated for a while
and the silence expanded
with night coming on.
Then I saw him one more time.
Half sunk into the haze of sunset,
he turned, made a great
exaggerated salute
and disappeared.

I stared at that small spot on the horizon
where he had stood.
I wondered what he would do
out there all night
with nothing in his pockets
but those old sheep bones,
and our final, bitter words.

My New Friend

all night the moon
tried to stay in my window

somewhere you were awake too
listening to your own voices
rummaging in the attic
like so many starving mice

my grass has gone to seed
and the neighbors
are getting up a petition
and a week from now
I will be in court
defending my right
to disappear and dream
with the shades closed
the doors swung open for air

the same air spinning in leaves
above your head

yesterday someone walked in
without knocking
someone not you
who wanted a drink
who wanted to press his face
into the dirty dishes
and speak of roots and ragweed
and the hollow ringing of church bells
down the alley

the roses have died
and the snakes are on my porch
but that means nothing to you
or to my new friend
who is asleep now
among the crusty forks and plates

Fun

A little boy and a woman
sit outside in the breezy sun.
He says something and they laugh
out loud. For me it's just a pantomime
through the window. Inside, I am

taking my coffee black today. Too hot.
If I complain, maybe they'll give
me a freebie. What are those
two up to, all that laughing
and touching. They lean in close.

The boy's eye catches mine
for a glance, then he turns quickly
back to her, saying something snide
I'm certain. I always make myself
perfectly presentable, so whatever

he says, it's a lie. And anyway, it's
unseemly for a woman and a boy
to be on such intimate terms
and right there in public. On my way
out, I stop at their table and look

at them. Pastry crumbs everywhere.
And does that porcelain cup mean she
let the boy drink coffee? I know they can
feel the power of self-control in my eyes.
"Good afternoon," I say. "Good

afternoon," they say in unison,
then look at each other in surprise.
The fools break into more laughter. Perfect,
I think, and wish that I'd said it.
When they don't invite me to join them,

I keep moving like always. I knew there was
something strange about those two.
I stand before my front door:
a flawless burgundy trimmed in grey.
Do I take out my keys and go in?
Or do I turn around and find another café?

Mentor

> for James Dickey

This giant, this man with a ten-gallon hat,
stands before the elevator, guitar case swinging
from the great mollusk of his hand.
Is it only the dead who can dwarf a door
while the rest of us swirl around him
like leaves in a creek around a boulder?
Is it only the dead who can break from the ocean
of my memory and crash back down again
for a dive to the deepest floor?

The loose bones of his bracelet crawl
over the seminar table. He announces
the rules: This is the living
room of the believable outrageous lie.
This is the crater of cracked dreams.
This is the predatory grace of a word
dropping on its prey from a branch. This is the poise
of a line that holds itself like the head of a snake.
This is the voice that fears not the guffaw
nor any cause of the guffaw.   He gathers the sentences
and dismembers them, scatters the fragments
across the page—the luminous bleached runes
of a dream, growing tooth by horn by tusk
into *my* dream. I too must become ruthless
to break him, break him down into noise,
into skin, into single words deprived
of the relevance of their kin, into one eye
bereft of the resonance of its twin.

On this final day of class he speaks
of the master archer, the arrows of the student
that will return again and again to kill him, to spill
his wild-ass, vainglorious blood into the sand,
into the red clay, into the deep-clawed roots.

Mud

The teacher's hand is alive in the garden.
No longer male or female, it resembles
the skin of mud, crawling slowly
like an ancient spider. We stay alert,
careful to hoe around it, to plant between
its fingers, and later to step over it
when picking the lettuce, the beets, the basil.

In the kitchen, we watch our own hands
slice tomatoes, squash, avocados,
into slender wheels, and we remember
the hand of the teacher, lounging
in the afternoon sun among beans,
cupping rain whether cold or warm,
encircling a weak sprout in the wind.

The Future

    on Van Gogh's *Wheatfield with Crows*

Did indigo strokes in blue sky
produce these crows?
Or did the crows, wheeling
from yellow wheat
like flying black widows, create
sky? The twin hard-packed
tracks curve into the distance
that may know. Green canopies
focus the blackness
of individual crows like lithe portals
looking into a world where sky
and crow are one. More crows
erupt from wheat around me.
More sky climbs into my eyes
until I cannot understand the past
that holds me to this red earth,
nor the present that hangs on the wire
of horizon
beyond which lurks everything I do not know
breaking up
into winged windows
looking more and more like crows.

Whirlwind

    for Harriet in the Bardo

I empty my heart but the husk is hard
I empty my mind but the body will not let go
of the way your flame carries on
in the emptiness of my rooms

if it were up to me
I would set you onto me again
you who have your own potent ghosts
a host of follower flames
that would keep me burning for years

while I sleep you are climbing a mountain
running your hands over the flowers
catching a glimpse of deer
that graze on those precipitous slopes

for a few days you walk alone
you let the rain come to you
your ghosts disintegrate
in the cold mountain streams
but your flame deepens like a rose

I know you won't return to me
I try not to be greedy
I savor the small fragrance of your hair
that remains
though it burns in my nostrils
like ripened dust

I must not suffer the loss of you
for the rest of my life
I must turn to other people
must test the scope of my heart

while what was once near
that I would still hold

rises up in a whirlwind of leaves
taking the form of your body
for just a moment

The Still Alive

1

In bed, your hand lies still, like a sleeping dog.
Touched, it moves and re-settles on the old
floppy pillow you've laid between us.

You've decided against loving the barrier
of trees. They are too tall, you say, blocking
your view of horizon on the distant hills.

But now a freezing rain keeps falling,
keeps thickening and breaking the limbs.
Your gaze begins to thaw within the window pane.

2

We cut and toss the fallen limbs, feet
among the grasses, leaves within our shirts,
fresh breeze in the still darkening sky.

An owl in a surviving tree dreams of night cries,
something that knows the labyrinths of ground.
Today the still alive turn back to what they know.

Tell your future children it was you who saved
these dramatic uprisings. Toss the pillow
to the floor. Lay your hand in mine among the sheets.

The Niche

a hand waves among trees
the flood recedes once again to the river
knifeblade stands in for horizon
white throat of the sky stalls
in one more forgettable utterance

the wave is real
slender white hand
sometimes a face among leaves
she wonders why you don't wave back
why you don't come to her

you retreat to some dark niche
a new book strokes your thighs
an ancient poem licks your heart
you shuffle the deck of faces
you fondle the dice
in the board game of beautiful bodies

after the flood there is fire in undergrowth
yearling trees wrenched and scorched
grow into troubling statements
the translations will go on forever
meanwhile you carry your book into woods
looking for a patch of sun

you find among torn branches
the small white bones
of a hand

Wild Man

>   for my first cousin Brad

Mostly eyes at birth, three months premature,
you weren't expected to live. The surrogate
mechanical womb they put you in did its job.
Son of a rich man, you grew up wild in the tiny

North Carolina town of Spruce Pine. Tall,
wiry, stubborn, smart, and a little bit crazy.
The cops could never catch you in your
supercharged, red Corvette on those winding

mountain roads. Without meaning to, you hit me
on the head twice: once with a baseball bat,
once with a golf club. Two years younger, I wanted
to be close to you, doing what you were doing.

You were the one who showed me magazines
of naked women. I was shocked and riddled
with strange desire. But in the end, I was
a dreamy poet looking for God, and you

were an ambitious CEO conquering markets.
Took over your father's tire business and made
millions. Loved a woman, loved your sons
and daughter, you were putty in the hands

of your grandchildren who climbed
all over you and outsmarted you every time.
Loved your guns too. Once, when drunk
in your basement on New Year's Eve, you fired

a line of bullets from your black market
submachine gun into the ceiling where
family and friends were partying above.
No one hit, no one hurt, you sold it the next day.

You loved your dogs, the land, the creeks
and rivers, and spent many days there.
On your last day, another New Year's Eve,
driving a remote road on the coast

of North Carolina near land you owned,
dogs' heads hanging out the windows,
cold wind battering your face,
the jeep got stuck in mud. You tried

to dig it out, to push it just far enough,
when your heart stopped. A stranger
found you lying there some hours later,
the dogs circling your body and barking

at the sun. Two months before that day,
you came to the funeral of my Harriet.
I was so glad to see you. You were sad
for me. And now, wild man, you too are gone.

Bullets

I don't know a single person here.
I met the artist once at a party. If someone
approaches me, I stare at my feet:
my toes are hiding something very

important. A person speaks to me
anyway. Her arms are slender, naked,
and I'm forced to look up from my toes glowing
with significance and meet her eyes:

I fall into her chiaroscuro
of possibilities—winding pathways,
doors left ajar, made beds sleek and shining.
Then, always, what I assume about others—

that they want my money, my time, my body,
my soul—rears its Hydra head and I look away.
My eyes land on a woman's hands mimicking
the brushstrokes of this abstract impressionist,

the yellow tuft of a little girl's head pressed
against her mother's leg, the very pointed toe
of an orange boot—everywhere except
those luminous thresholds where a thousand

futures lurk, invaded by every shameful bias
and hope of my overactive mind. My eyes
glance off of hers like bullets off of Godzilla.
Thank God for this bizarre art hanging on the wall.

My eyes can rest like birds in those amorphous
intricacies. I can speak of what I pretend
to believe the painting means: the un-
certainty of life, the power of dreams,

the desire to meet, and be met. Boredom
rises into her eyes like a fever.
And soon I'm alone again to contemplate
the half-heartedness of the moon in this painting.

Yes, I'm sure it's a moon, its roundness
morphed into sharp angles like the flash of an eye,
half in darkness, half in light, with something
like rifles gleaming in the nearby hills.

One Wish

Every morning I step on the back porch
and breathe out a spinning cone of air.
My small dog scrambles under shrubs
and comes up snorting and shaking,
thin string of drool across his snout.
The day parcels out these minutes

one at a time till nothing is left
but the booze-darkness of sleep.
When I first started thinking like this
I was a young man planning to grab
one of these years by the throat
and choke it into howling submission,

as if the world might lay anything down
at my feet besides some windblown trash.
When I first started drinking, I wanted
to show myself that it was nothing,
that it was just one more way to spend myself
under the sidewalk moon of July.

But this is no self-pitying compilation
of complaints, no blank sheet of paper
filling itself up with sorry scratchings of the sad life.
I love that full bottle waiting for me
under the sink among the sponges.
I love the backyard domain that my scraggily mutt

rules. This is only a wish, undeserved I know,
to keep on waking up with nothing to say
to anyone but my dog. The morning moon
has no trouble finding me through the cottonwood
that has thrown down most of its leaves.
The cold, sweet air from an old river has no trouble.

Seizure

    for Paula Goff

They found you on the floor
of your mobile home, stacks
of newspapers rising around you
like the skyscrapers of some lost city
and you the fetal river overflowing

your banks, flooding the streets.
I began to lose you when you fell
in love with the great poet, believing
in his shamanic power to transform you
into the white owl of a legendary wood.

He penetrated your dreams—
guided you into luminous landscapes
where white bears and TV anchors
met for lunch over giant schooners of ale,
where spiritual elevators lifted you

into realms of shimmering light,
where the words of the great poet
plunged to the earth of heaven, bolted
into the primeval forest, preening
with eternal wolverines and lions and eagles.

When I first met you, we too made
a connection, performed psychic
experiments, your damp back pressed
against mine next to the fountain,
writing those first poems and stories

as if our lives depended on them.
But the shaman poet hired you to be
his assistant, and then you sat with him
and stood and walked with him
and disappeared into the night with him,

until your face morphed into his face,
the cool flame behind your eyes
swelling into the fire behind his,
the cadences of your poems locking
step with the cadences of his. Every night

you wandered in the astral plain
with him, claiming the animal heavens,
the psychic wormholes of human pain.
When he drank himself to death in 1997,
you flew even deeper into the wild depths

to find him. I know now that you were lost
only to your own choices, and so
not lost at all, free to spend each day
poring over the back-page articles
for clues, studying cop shows and soaps

for signs of the hidden story behind
each face and act you dreamed,
while I was bound by duty and boss.
You were happiest when you could tip
the bottle back and let the glory flow,

your mind stunned into awe by the light
lashing every cell of your brain.
If one of us was lost, it was I,
believing that I somehow knew
how someone should live her life.

My telephone records show your last
call to me came the day before the day
they found your devastated body,
your voice on my machine slurring words
into a river sliding over boulders

where the white owl and the white bear
meet in their ancient mission.
I love you, you said, then laughed.
I didn't return your excited call, left you
to feel the surge of that final seizure.

In the Flesh

1

why do they
      reject me
or at least
      not bring me
into the fold

they freeze me out

      hold me
in my disappointment

      they say
something small
      they didn't intend
maybe didn't have a clue
      what it would mean
to me

          so what am I doing
what face am I making
      what tone of voice
      do I project
that means they must reject me

I think I want
      to see myself in action
        to diagnose

how do I turn
in order to see myself
to see what is wrong with me

         if they love me
      if they welcome me
even then I always know
they are playing me

time
      will reveal it
but I know it
already

2

if I just keep walking
        people disappear
                behind me
others suddenly appear
before me

who is it that sees so clearly

the streets
        have been repaired
smooth black shiny patches
where warped blacktop
and holes used to be

some windows
        have bold closed curtains
like plays that never begin
        but overall
things are about the same

time follows me
                precedes me
    or jumps inside my skin
and then I fall
        asleep
or wake up   and it's not
        things
that are the same
        but me

time has walked
                in my shoes
and thought my thoughts
and laughed
        my laughs
that I could use
           right about   now

now that I know
time is
      like my smell
invisible aura
        spiraling
             around me

3

pain coils
inside   hot bulb
burning in my gut
if I stay alone
it grows like a
snake trapped
in a bottle and if
I go outside   it
chokes the life out
of trees and people
and any conversation
will be with the dead
and thus I allow my
self no leeway
with eyes
          neither
mine nor theirs

and instead I
look away I carry
my pain past
everyone and into
the forest where
I can lie down
on a bed of needles
and the bulb
inside flares white
hot and soon I
will be to blame
                these
trees full of
        birds
will be burning

4

    who said what
                to whom
    when and where

    did I say it   was it
                  me
    or is it just the
               state
    of the nation
    the state of the gut
    of the room of the eye

    of the man who
                did
    say what he said

    and on cue I broke
    open

        my body like the peel
    of an orange
         penetrated by thumbs
    and let the insect
              of his
                   word
    crawl in
    and bury its head

    in my flesh

    and I knew
               I cannot live like this

5

I fell asleep
time passed
and when I woke
the word's hold
on the flesh of my heart
had broken
was I the one who broke it

the word turned toward me
its jaws still gaping and bloody
I saw it for the first time
its face was mine

I commanded it

its segmented black legs churned
down a wooded path
inside my body
I followed it
to a stony creek
where it lay down   died
and plummeted away like a leaf
on white water

I had cut
a course in my body
for that word to crawl out

for all the words
that wound me
to crawl out

and be carried away
on the creek
that runs beside me
or is it within me

let's say it is
running within and without
me
and that it keeps taking away

what I do not need
so that I can talk with you
I can listen
I can hear what you are saying

your words cannot
hurt me

not for long anyway

my hands are not
balling into fists
my shoulders are not trying
to form wings to escape
into the high safe canopies

instead
                I stay here
                              in my body
my feet in the dirt
      the mask of your face
            opens like curtains
      to show your real face
and the play begins

The Grip

> for my mother

The oxygen machine shoots out another puff,
and my mother takes another breath
from the tube in her nose. Her eyes open,
a subtle smile rising in her resigned face
when she sees me. The TV flickers
and she straightens up in her recliner
to watch her favorite macho crime buster,

Chuck Norris, pursue—this time—a slick,
black-suited, thug-protected, drug lord.
But her eyes wander, and she doesn't see
Chuck whirl another karate kick to a hooligan head.
Instead, her eyes come to rest on the clown
puppet astride the top shelf of her bookcase.
She doesn't dwell on the overlarge

red smile, the blue exclamatory eyes.
Instead, her eyes turn inward to the scene
she has described to me many times before:
the arthritic hands of the shopkeeper
rake the puppet down from a display
and set it vividly upright on the counter—
that brash splash of color and gangly cloth—

and my mother reaches into its body
for the hidden grip, makes its wooden shoes
dance on the counter, makes its stuffed head
bob to a tune she sings, and the gap-toothed
old shopkeeper claps and laughs.
As a kid of five, I'd run into my parents' room,
pull that jester down and find the inner

grip, make it dance, make it tell the jokes
I'd heard my mother tell but didn't
understand, make it sing to the dog
who'd run and hide behind the couch
wild-eyed until she placed the puppet back
on its perch. From her mother dimension
high among the fluorescent lights, she

coached me through the solar system of house,
over thresholds into the galaxy of backyard,
through the gate into the universe of town and beyond.
My mother's eyes surface to the here and now,
pass over the credits rising on the TV screen,
settle on my face. Her dying eyes find my living eyes—
take hold, gently, of the well-worn grip inside.

Learning to Speak

Tired of the sound
of my own voice—
my complaints lining up
like dolls on the headboard

of a child's bed—I placed
my mouth in a jewel box.
What is the world
without my crown of words?

My rooms grew quiet
around me. My eyes
reached through windows
to passing cars and windy trees.

I held my hand out to the front
door like an old friend
I hadn't seen in years.
Outside, I saw a solo maple leaf

sashay on the breeze,
heard the call of a single crow
swaying on the highest limb
of an oak. My neighbor

raking her front yard
smiled at my soundless nod.
A boy on his bike grew
wide-eyed at the spectacle

of smooth vacant skin above
my chin. Explanations
thrummed within my throat.
When a friend asked me

where my mouth had gone,
I formed letters with my hands,
but he shook his head, no time
to spare for reading. I walked to town

and saw in each person I met
the grooved path of their
racing mind, saw the dark
current of their heart. Silent,

I walked back home,
closed my door against the light.
The phone lay still as an egg.
I found the jewel box

and the scowl that was my mouth
twisted like a dirty shirt inside.
I ran it through a cycle
of hot on hot. I heated up

the steam iron and pressed it
straight. I planted it on my face,
a neutral, thin line waiting
for the next impulse. At first,

I coughed without mercy.
I screamed, I laughed, I cursed,
I made pronouncements
I'd never thought before: The truth

is a lie in its past and future
lives. The monkeys of November
are the talking heads of June.
The old words and the new

queued up on the windowsill
and the headboard,
a thousand tiny somebodies
with moving mouths.

Each one, gnarly
as an old parakeet, craved
equally to speak the facts,
and to tell the story.

The Lairs

Your White Shoes

    for Robert Dana

1

One night after we'd all had
too much Jack, you fell
on the steep trail going
down to your door,
your white shoes suspended
briefly in the grainy darkness
above your head. As I
helped you up,
half falling myself
on the slippery grass,
your shoes glowed
in the moon shadow
of an ancient magnolia.
When you went back home to Iowa,
you left those white shoes for me.

2

In a small schoolyard in Peru
I played my first game of soccer
on a team of white foreigners
against a team of mestizos
and another of Quechua Indians.
Their play was rough and fast
and full of laughter.
We had to buy the beer,
and even drunk
they beat us again.
The beer in tall liter bottles
was cheap and good. The doors
of the cinder block school
were open, rooms
empty except for blackboards.
I understood few of their words,
but knew their laughter was for us,
Americans who played their best
and still could not win a game.
As darkness fell, we broke up
with friendly high fives all around,

washing our beat-up bodies
two or three at a time
in a spring gushing up from a pipe.
They headed for their chores
among the packhorses
or for their homes in the village.
Their children played in our camp,
curious and shy,
gathering around anyone
with a flashlight
and an open book.
I headed for my tent
and a cup of hot coca tea,
happy and sad and tired,
your battered white shoes
caked with dust and sweat.

3

Like your poems, your white shoes—
worn to mottled grey and creased
across the toes—are still good
around the house, and in the yard,
and out on the trail. Out there,
an adolescent maple
catches small currents,
slides them through the palms
of its leaves like fine silk.
Cloven hooves punctuate
the black earth, the passages
quoted full of white-throated sparrows
and white-tailed deer.
A pileated woodpecker
hammers the bark in search
of carpenter ants. The creek
unwinds its tangled statement
into the river.
A blue concerto swells in the canopy.
I stand very still in your white shoes.
An "ordinary rain begins to fall."

The Garden

remember them
it should not be difficult
they are not old coins in dusty jars
they are children
marched out in a parade
by their captors

watch them lift
a severed hand from the curb
knowing it by the calluses
or the ring
watch them hold
a hollow face to their chest

walk out into the storm
of singing shrapnel
and when you come back
you won't forget the torn
thrown into streets like game
as you belly-up to the table

tomorrow they will take
your face in their hands
will press your eyes
with their own
for answers you don't
know how to give

for they haven't yet turned
the flesh and bones
burned in great pyres
into a new heart
sharp as chiseled stone
haven't yet dreamed

the blood
of their dead
into their own veins
as one cannot make use right away
of all the fallen leaves
in the garden

Dead Ringer

    for my father

I dream of crying in my father's
office. The tall windows shatter.
Tiny shards sting my face.
Vines reach in and hug the wall
so tight the paint cracks. The ceiling
groans and sags. Rows
of fluorescent lights blink and hum.
On his desk, debris litters a new
house plan, ranch style, that will never
be built.   I wake up dry-eyed,
sitting in a room full of mourners.
Outside, toddlers peel their clothes
off in the water sprinkler,
play naked in the horseshoe pit.
Fitting tribute, somebody says,
children playing where your father drank
a thousand whisky sours and threw
a thousand ringers with a thousand shouts.
Friends, relatives, and strangers
hug me, mumble in my ear
how proud of me he'd been,
how much like him I am. I wander
outside and into the woods until
the noise of voices crumbles into leaves.
I want only the random eyes of trees,
inscrutable, requiring nothing of me.
It's summer and I lie down
in the creek in my dark suit. I listen
to the rocks knocking together
under the surface like the rummaging
of thieves in an old man's
house.   I must be dreaming again. Wet
and sleek as an otter, I stand up,
walk deeper into the woods until
I emerge on a road of no houses,
only the unbroken rows of trees
for many miles. I hitchhike to Utah

and walk into a canyon in the desert,
find a cave where I can be alone.
I study this absence of the tears I want to cry.
It's not that I hate my father, not
that I won't miss him. I build a small
fire, flames projecting animal shadows
on the chiseled walls, enticing moths
from the mouth of a night
so black even nocturnal predators
stumble and fall.
                    But I have to wake up,
stagger out of this cave, and admit
that I have done none of this. I shake
myself awake and greet a few more
mourners. Then I head for a door
and lock myself into my father's room,
his office away from office, press
my forehead onto a photo of the two
of us—side by side and grinning
at my sister's wedding—and try to imagine
a tear I could present to others, the feel
of it on my lid and lashes, rolling
down my face, the salt taste of it
on my tongue. I try to remember
some earlier tear I have manufactured—
at a marriage or a wake—but I cannot
escape the unmoving fact of his
turned back, disappearing car, closed door.
As I grew into my teens, he taught me
always to be coiled to strike, if necessary.
In that scenario, tears are not allowed.
From beyond his freshly occupied grave,
my father appears in his leather chair,
pushes his hair back like JFK, his face
a mixture of disappointment and pride.
One more time, as in the old days, I sit across
from him and speak, tell him
that I'm a man now who knows
some things that he will never know.

He slaps the arm of his chair and laughs.
His eyes tell me he knows not only
what I know, but a whole lot more besides.
The dead know everything, he says.
I wake again to my own laughter,
a drunken fool with my forehead pressed
against the damp glass covering our two
faces, guffawing my guts out until tears fall
and make a small puddle on the rug.
In the solitude behind my father's locked door,
with somber yet giddy mourners partying
on the other side, I step through my father's
secret exit to the back yard. The kids
have all dried and dressed and gone inside.
I take my stance just as my father taught me:
feet apart, knees slightly bent, shoulders
leaning forward, right hand holding
before my face the cold broken circle,
eyes focused on the metal stake
forty feet away. I step into it, this
thrust, this final throw, feeling the balanced
release as it flies in a perfect tumbling arc
into one last clank of iron on iron.

Mr. Reflex Man

I don't remember when
he set his face in my window pane at night
so that even my dreams belong to him.
He bought my eyes and the tone
of my voice for a tuneless song,
the soles of my feet that could not bear
to walk on rocks or the hot blacktop
for a pair of old, argyle socks.
He encircled me with concerns
until his words were the only ones,
the wounds I absorbed like minerals.
He forced his hands inside of mine,
snapped the skin tight like rubber gloves.

He said listen to your father and mother,
listen to your teachers.
It doesn't matter that they are right and wrong.
They will give you what you want
if you are weak when they are strong
and strong when they are weak.

He said, never mind me. I don't require
your attention or your generous support.
I have staked out territory in every cell
of your body. I tighten your throat
when you start to speak. I sharpen
the precise tremor of your hands
when you stand to make an important
point. I am the small sign slapped
on your back by a grinning friend that says
touch me and I'll knock your head off,
speak to me and I'll turn away, weeping.
He said, I offer all of this protection
and much more, and you will never know
I'm here, lurking just behind your left ear.

Headless

> It took me no time at all to notice that this nothing, this hole
> where a head should have been was no ordinary vacancy, no
> mere nothing. On the contrary, it was very much occupied.
> —Douglas Harding, *On Having No Head*

1

If I look down and cross my eyes,
I can see the side of my nose, my nostril flaps.
If I push my lips up, the white hairs
of my mustache appear, but my beard
is out of sight. If I blow up my cheeks
they rise into view like twin moons
on the horizon. Even the tip of my tongue
if I work at it, and the curved bill
of my cap drawing the world slightly
into focus. Not to mention the sensations
I feel when wiggling my ears or blinking.
All solid evidence of my head. And if I
bring my hands up, I can feel the wish
of my jaw and the Oh-bones around my eyes.

2

But I get what he meant when he said he had
no head. I can't see what is seeing, which is where
my head should be. I have never actually seen
my face. But I can see the uncorked bottle
of wine, the empty glass, the joined photos
of my Harriet and me, the light curved against the wall
by the lamp shade, the partially read Sunday comics,
and outside my window, the stunningly still
cherry tree just beginning to blossom, the full
birdfeeder hanging untouched by bird in the dusk,
one sparrow chipping for the night to come on,
for the light farther away but as sure as anything
we think we know. I see darkening sky, a dim star,
and deadly blue space. Who is it, what is it,

that sees all of this and more, but says not a thing?

Let It Come

>   for my sister Patti

1

Seven years older than I, beautiful,
and I couldnt understand why boys
were always arriving at the house
and sitting beside you on the couch.
I hid behind the big chair, and when
the kissing started, I bombed you two
with rolled-up socks from the laundry.

The first time, you screamed and chased
me around the living room, laughing.
The second time, you got pissed off
and landed a good slap to my face.
The third time, you allowed the bombs
to fall on your kissing without reaction,
leaving Mother to do the dirty work.

2

But you were the one who did the dirty work
when Mother got old, had surgery on her spine
and heart, had to be on oxygen all the time.
You were her best friend, took her shopping,
out to lunch, sat beside her for hours each day.

Not much for women friends, you were a lover
of men to the end, even when they did you wrong,
a lover of sex and food and good drink. You quit
smoking and walked three miles a day, but it was
too late. The beast sank its claws in you and you

fought it best you could, until at last you told
the doctors to fuck themselves, and declined
further treatment. Let it come, you told your
daughters, let whatever it is please come on to me.

Hooks

From here, through this window
overlooking the street, I can see the sky
searching, losing
its focus on the day.

And I'm rising, climbing
like a leaf caught in an updraft,
till I'm standing on the highest corner
of a ten-story hotel
abandoned a decade ago,

how I love these journeys,

ghost-wanderers asleep
beneath my feet, resting in the routines
of chewing tobacco and hairspray,
seeing the same movie they saw
in the last town, lots of chases
and embraces, alone
with the unshared comfort of popcorn.

Like everyone, I rise even higher into the cloud
where I become giant eyes
turning, the child of storms

overlooking the maze of this big town
neither white nor full of light
but mottled with the colors
of something living and dying
at the same time,

moving like a mirrored sky
or like the lost love waving her hand
as she drives away.

I hope she is spirit-deep
into some new escapade
full of daring and survival
and the grace of a good drink
or a long, transforming embrace.

From here, I see a cat sleeping
in the constant shade
of a sleek, abandoned Buick.
I see an ancient carp in the river
laughing at the dangling hooks—

the visible ones, anyway.

Lines of Sight

    for Steve Gardner

Older than I by months,
what were you doing in those first
days and weeks
while I still curled up in the burrow
of my mother's womb?

Planting your small fist
in the palm of your cop father's hand,
letting him spread the coil of your fingers
to count the possible years
in barely formed lines?

Maybe waking in the darkness
of your mother's arms and feeling
home again,
tucked away from the edges
of those first hurled words
and the flux of eyes and hands.

We grew in parallel worlds
eighty miles apart—
our newfound voices sparked
under different loblolly pines of the same night.
Our eyes fielded splinters of light
from the same stars.

You were the one who taught me
about The Cream and Three Small Faces,
who listened to my words as if they mattered.
You took me into your home
when I didn't know where home was
and made a pallet in a corner
where I could stretch my body out and sleep
like a man who had discovered something
everyone could use.

We shuffled the words in those days
like cards from an endless deck.
The chimes of your Nancy's laughter
rang in the wind of our debates.
Your friends already knew my name
when I met them. We gathered in your house
to talk Nam and Ginsberg and Malcolm X.
Your surveyor neighbor
paid me to follow him deep
into red-clay forests
carrying his tripods and levels,
setting up lines of sight.

But it's you I keep seeing,
red-bearded and long-haired,
squinting that mysterious smile
that cracks into wild, high-pitched laughter,
veins of smoke from the pipe
spiraling above your head.

It's just you and me on this night.
The black dog Stokely Carmichael
nestles beside you on the couch.
His eyes follow you
even through closed lids,
follow that long-fingered hand
that could palm a basketball
or balance a Milk Bone on his nose.

That same hand—red-freckles,
rash of psoriasis, crooked little finger—
reaches out to me and breaks—
like bread—the silence
that has grown between us.

At Night

The man under your bed
owns one knife for many purposes.
When hungry he opens a blade and watches
street light from the window play on its surface.
He spits on his reflection and draws

the blade over the blue cuff of his shirt—
the knife given to him by his father
on a February day years ago
deep in the woods made silent by falling snow,
each flake the size of a silver dollar.

The man under your bed
will give you old toenail clippings,
photos you hid under the mattress and forgot,
the chewed-up collar of a long dead dog,
but the man will not show you his red-handled knife

and the many blades folded like the feet
of a seagull tucked away in flight.
He has taken your gloves from the bottom drawer
and stroked his own face with that foreign skin,
has taken your shoes and pulled the laces tight.

All night he follows the currents of dust,
fishes for coins he does not know how to spend,
studies the word *sleep* which he can speak
in a dozen languages but cannot define.
He smiles as he did years ago

when someone came to him in the night.
But that was before he found his true path:
he must stay awake while you sink into darkness,
he must feel the cracks between boards,
the debris of daylight washed up on the shore of your room.

Speech Minus Applause

I am taking a break from this world.

I don't open any of the day's correspondence,
gathered like mulberry leaves under the mail slot.

In my yard I study the ice-white branches
of cottonwoods. I listen carefully to voices
sliding through cracks in my privacy fence.
In the back alley I follow all the deflections
of sunlight against dumpsters.

Weed seeds stick to the cuffs of my jeans,
ride my flying feet to some promised land.

The lies I haven't told yet
coalesce in my exploratory thoughts.
A cold drizzle clings like spit to my face.

The streets would all have me believe
that they are full of small round stones
clicking against each other in ocean surf
but I know it is only rubber hitting the road.

And the windows of the houses around here
present their roving silhouettes as if to say
the lives being lived in this neighborhood alone
are as pointless as the leaves still hugging
their limbs in the cold fall breezes.
But I know that a man is not a leaf.

And the children who draw their hopscotch courses
with colorful pieces of chalk on the sidewalk
and skip on one foot according to mindless rhymes
would have me absolutely convinced
that they were born today, that they have never
drawn the night around them and breathed it in.

But I know better,
I know a child is already one of us
when she cries out with her first breath.

The Lairs

At the community market
people stroll among the vendors' stalls
selling eatles and pieport sets, plaques
with baseballs plugging the "O" of "LOVE,"
patchwork quilts, gleaming wooden
bowls and birdhouses, Helga's
knitted hats and Evelyn's hooded
towels. Laughing kids hold
the hands of older siblings.

Each person is an object
in my awareness, and I am
an object in theirs. When I wake up
here, a presence among presences,
they are more than just objects,
something imbedded and burning
in them, as it burns in me. Or
is that only my imagination?
Am I adding something that isn't there?

For years I crawled in my own muck
and spouted useless hot air, a dying bird
gathering dust in the gutter. But ants
and worms have dissolved the carcass,
carried it into millions of lives and deaths.
The clouds keep on hiding and revealing
the sun without putting on airs.

It's easier now to remain as what remains
when the light itself keeps shedding
its own accumulated lairs.

The Final Days

>   for myself

The sun slides out
of a slot of clouds
beyond the pine horizon.

Misty layers of undergrowth
draw the eye deeper in
where roots and boulders mingle.

Above the tallest spire, a smoky white line
breaks apart, falling
             and the first low voices seep
from nearby windows just now.
They crawl the way only voices can
from porches and driveways
up the road and beside the creek
gone almost dry—where rocks
can hear them, also bird droppings
among leaves.

A pair of pileated woodpeckers
guffaw back and forth
and I'm lying here in this hammock
where the sun grows clear and smaller
and piercing to the eye.

A pale slice of moon floats remotely
on the other side of sky. Distant dogs
announce certain mysterious arrivals:

deer push their faces through foliage
and step out one by one onto grass,
listen together
to all the small, sudden noises;

old mothers turn silent and graceful
in their grazing. Yearlings play
or lie down in wet grass warming in the sun.

My heart loses itself out there
among the impermanent but particular ones
where I sometimes walk alone and dream
of the final days of this life and what they may bring.

In Defense of Permanence

If everything is impermanent
as the Buddha says,
then the light of permanence swells
inside your hands
preparing your face for the day
in the mirror that reverses you.
Later, you lift the slice towards your mouth
as if it were the first apple.
If all phenomena are impermanent
then permanence plants a seed
in everything dead or alive—
my father long gone into leukemia's
lair, my mother into the burnt
air of radiated lungs, my sister
into the smoke she kissed good-bye
too late, my beloved into the slow
erosion of glioblastoma.
      The permanence of impermanence
establishes the blue of your eyes
at 10:08 a.m. at the community table
outside Irene's Country Kitchen.
They gaze at the day as if it were a page
made for the turning, the night as if it were
an open house priced to sell. Your nameless
sheep graze in the fields where each blade
is as nameless and numberless
as the witnessing eyes of permanence.
Who sees the carefully named children
playing among the feet of great oaks
in the park? They themselves change
into watchful parents. Your body
will become ash, it's true, and your ashes
flying dust, yes, but the wind
is a long exhalation of the one who sees.

Prelude to a Move

My sister brought it out
from the safe in the cellar.
The lights had flickered out days before,
the cold had seeped into the walls.
She carried it beneath her robe
pressed against the skin of her belly—
that grotesquely beautiful stone
that robbed even the moonless midnight
of every speck of light.
She turned to fix me with her desperate eyes
before she closed her door.

Years later a tall butler
held it aloft on a gold platter
among the patter of polite applause
and placed it in the center of my sister's palm
before she slipped into the limo
beside her rich lover,
rice raining against the black sheen,
the smile on her face waning
in the rear window.

More years later a stooped messenger
chaperoned it from a faraway land.
He didn't speak my language
and I couldn't read his eyes
behind that drooping hat,
yet still he reached the stone out
wrapped in a dirty scrap of paper
that held a few words I couldn't understand
for the letters were like none I'd seen
and may not have been letters at all
but only small splatters made by a child,
and when I turned back to the messenger
he'd slipped away with the stone
and a pair of my best gloves.

Much later a henchman
in a three-piece suit escorted it
in a steel-reinforced briefcase
from the house of my sister's husband
with papers I had to sign
promising to make certain sacrifices
of a personal kind,
and when I wouldn't
he ushered the package away
as if to say the skin of his own nose
would not be threatened.

One day five years later at dusk
it was delivered in the back of a truck
protected by tarps.
Two large men lowered it to my lawn
with long straps,
then they drove away fast.
How could the stone have grown so large?
I couldn't lift it alone,
couldn't get it into my house,
and the next morning it was gone,
the soft grass stamped by deep footprints
and cut by tires.

Finally a friend of my sister
in a summer dress and white stockings
delivered it in a flourish,
with hands so perfect they made
my own hands ache.
She said that my sister was sorry
she couldn't bring it herself,
stuck as she was in a borderless country.

I carried the small unwrapped box
into my stale house and shut all the doors.
My sister's friend still stood on the lawn
and studied my windows,
hoping to catch my eye I think,
the way a woman searches out
the eyes of her potential lover.
I closed all the blinds and curtains.

When I opened the box,
it revealed a small bronze arrow
emblazoned with my name.
It kept changing its direction.
What had happened to the great stone?
I heard my sister's beautiful friend
laughing beneath my window.

Karma

1

You are
the way you channel the chicken and rice into the grin on
your face, the arch of your brows, the shifting current of
skin around cheekbones.

You are
the way you say your name, the way you draw air through
lungs and throat and over the vocal folds, in the way you
curve your tongue, touch it to the roof of your mouth, pin it
between your teeth with the air escaping around it, spinning
the tone of what you think about yourself.

The way too
that you hold the bow of yourself—with confidence or
uncertainty—how you pull the arrow of your intent notched
into the string—arms shaking, or flowing smoothly with the
extension—how you sight down the shaft—the timing of
your release with the instroke of your heart, with the
outward thrust of your breath—is you.

There is revelation
in the way you conduct your hands as you speak, in the way
you cup and lift and slice and box and grapple the air, in the
way you charge the space with the gestures of your spell, as
if your hands were the engine under the hood of your voice.

Not that what you say
is true or false, but that how you say it reveals the sparks
from old wounds and caresses that ignite the blood in your
heart and brain. Not that any of this is really you—the one
who turns to see it, the one beyond the reach of wounds and
caresses.

2

    You are a hat, made in a factory in the Mid-West with tens of thousands of brethren, bearing the cut and fortitude of your design, shipped in the amniotic packaging of great boxes within the holds of semis to stores at the coast, in the mountains, and on the plains.

    Still, you are yourself, made more so by the way your owner chooses you, separates you from the stack of those below and above you by the color of your crown. By the way he grasps your bill to put you on and take you off, imparting a certain angle, a certain twist. By the way he tosses you spinning onto the dresser before making love. By the way he scrapes through the underbrush holding you on with one hand, by the way his sweat stains your skull. One day he hangs you on a rack, piling other clothes on top of you, until he forgets where you are, as so much else has been lost and forgotten in a long life.

    In the weeks and months that pass, you steep in silence, never one to talk in any case. You make peace with the cold weight of a leather jacket, the stink of an old sweatshirt, the wasted usefulness of a dog leash. You dream a fall above those sweatshirted shoulders chopping wood. A winter drifting above the warmth embraced by that jacket. A spring following the dog into crazy underbrush.

    When he finds you in the heat of summer, you are still not the self that you never were. You are cloth and leather and metal clasp. You sense the pleasure he takes in discovering you. He spins you around and around on the upturned spider of his hand, re-shapes you with his fist, pulls you onto his head, adjusts the clasp. Your vision snaps to life in his eyes. You turn when he turns. If he falls, you go down with him. You ride outside, a witness to leaves and sky. You dance in the soles of his feet.

What You Know

> for Jerry Phillips

It sounds crazy, but I lost track of my best friend.
We didn't live close to each other, but we
sometimes met halfway and traveled to the coast
or the mountains. We'd sit across from each

other and argue philosophy, religion, politics.
My emails, phone messages, and last resort
snail mail to him all went unanswered
for months. My queries of mutual friends

led nowhere. At last I took a day off
and drove to my friend's city only to find
his house abandoned and occupied
by a band of feral cats, no forwarding address.

Heading back home, exhausted, I pulled
off the road and parked among weeds, thinking
my friend did not want to be found,
not by me anyway. I wondered what

I had done to cause him to leave without
a word: something I said in a letter taken
the wrong way, that must be it. But how could I
correct this mistake now that I couldn't

find him? I woke up in the middle
of the night full of the absence of my friend's
remarkable face, his furrowed brow, the bulbous
nose, the wit of incredulity always lurking

behind those pale blue eyes. I was sick
with the absence of my friend's dismissive
hand gestures, the sketchbook in his lap, his tales
of Egypt and the God Horus, the fierce stubbornness

of his opinions, his generosity with money
and his disturbing portraits. I had fallen asleep
in my car, and I rolled the window down
for a breath of night air. A pair of owls called

deep in the woods. The light of a cloudless full moon
lay down on the lined highway like the bankless
body of a river. By that light, I saw
my friend standing in the middle of the road

with his head cocked to one side, his clothes
hanging old and worn on his body, his eyes full
of tears at the sight of his own lost friend. I blinked
and blinked, and he disappeared like a possum

scuttling into underbrush. I want this to be a night
like that one, old friend, only better, with you really
showing up on my doorstep in such glorious light
after a long journey to a place my inquiries

cannot reach. Please come in and sit down
in the best chair, have a drink of the best whisky
money can buy, and report on what you've seen.
Criticize me, please. Tell me what you know.

The Way It Is

As the night sharpens its knives
        on the fabric of the North Atlantic
        beyond the cliffs of this old fortress,
        I remember myself.
        I stroll among the black and white dancers.
        I descend the stairs
        to corridors beneath their gamboling feet
        that lead to the catacombs.
        The cacophony of their waltzes and polkas
        breaks again and again
        on the shores of deep cathedrals.
        I touch each corpse in its black chamber
        and I remember myself.

As the night lays its cold news over the continent,
        I turn away from a face, a hand
        reaching out, a voice
        spiraling among the doors,
        a call from so far away
        it defines the grey line of horizon,
        and I remember myself,
        a white duck in the rain
        longing for something cold on my skin,
        a small strong voice in my ear saying
        risk it now, saying *dive*
        while the sun rides on the other side of darkness.

As the night throws its massive skull back and laughs
        at the million-headed joke of the comedian
        flickering into the cracks of walls,
        the joints of furniture and old men,
        I remember myself,
        how the laugh grows inside of me
        like the slow-rising burn from a shot of Jack,
        like the smoldering spark of the fuse
        darting through blades of grass
        toward the inner neighborhood—
        a promise of the great nothing
        while everything around me tenses
        into complicated forms.

As the night speaks its last blue vowels among the flowers,
    someone whispers her red answer under the yellow moon
    and her lover's hand touches her thigh.
    I walk in the grove watching the flight
    of dry leaves in this cutting wind,
    and I remember myself, loverless
    and alone like one long note
    of music in the night, interrupted
    by breathing, just breathing
    among the sheets.

As the night gives up its black ghost
    to the gray one bleeding on its sleeves,
    I remember myself
    on the other side of a wall
    where the nameless people know me
    as I know them,
    bodies of whirling light.
    I remember myself—
    I stand in this plain room
    reflected in a mirror,
    my unexpected form staring
    wide-eyed at me
    like the black bear
    I startled last November
    in the woods.

As the night withdraws its tentacles from the Pacific,
    coiling them into storage
    in the dark cellars of clouds,
    I remember myself.
    My right hand makes a fist
    and buries itself in the left.
    My past gathers its unbreakable threads
    and burning stones.
    I drag them into the long day,
    allow them to stretch out behind me in procession,
    certain I am myself—and everything I see.

Epilogue

MINERALS

I long to find

in the eyes of one man

or woman

that fierce calm—

the silence of one

sunk so deeply

into roots

her long-awaited words

climb like minerals

into high leaves

rising

through all the circles

of atmosphere

into the cold

condensations

of morning.

Cover artist Jim Muehlemann is a recipient of the Prix de Rome from the American Academy in Rome. He has also received a grant from the Adolph and Ester Gottlieb Foundation. Prior to the professorship that he now holds at Randolph College, Jim lived in New York City for twenty years, where he had numerous one-person exhibitions. He continues to show his work throughout the country. Jim lives with his wife Kathy in Lynchburg, Virginia.

Jim Peterson was born in Augusta, Georgia, reared and educated on the banks of the Savannah River in western South Carolina. His poetry collections include *The Man Who Grew Silent, An Afternoon With K, The Owning Stone, The Bob and Weave,* and *Original Face*. His novel, *Paper Crown*, is now available on Audible. His poems have won the Benjamin Saltman Award from Red Hen Press, an Academy of American Poets Award, and a Fellowship in Poetry from the Virginia Arts Commission. A number of his plays have been produced in regional theaters. Until his retirement in 2013, he was Coordinator of Creative Writing at Randolph College and was the Pearl S. Buck Writer-in-Residence there in the Fall of 2017. Many years ago, he was founder and editor of the poetry journal *Kudzu* and later was editor of *The Devil's Millhopper* poetry magazine and press. He is now on the faculty of the University of Nebraska-Omaha Low-Res MFA Program in Creative Writing and is professor emeritus at Randolph College in Lynchburg, Virginia, where he lives with his charismatic corgi, Mama Kilya.

www.ingramcontent.com/pod-product-compliance
Lightning Source LLC
LaVergne TN
LVHW041343080426
835512LV00006B/602